S0-CID-935

# Nature's Children

## FARM BIRDS

### by Edward C. Haggerty

Grolier Educational

# FACTS IN BRIEF

**Classification of farm birds.**

|  |  |
|---|---|
| Class: | *Aves* (birds) |
| Order: | *Galliformes* |
| Family: | *Phasianidae* (chickens and turkeys); *Anatidae* (ducks and geese) |
| Species: | *Gallus gallus* (chicken); *Meleagris gallopavo* (turkey); *Anos platyrhynchos* (ducks); *Anser anser* (domestic goose); *Branta canadensis* (Canada goose) |

**World distribution.**   Geese, ducks, and chickens raised everywhere; turkeys raised mostly in North America and Europe.

**Habitat.**   Wild ducks and geese near bodies of water; wild turkeys, upland wooded areas; chickens domesticated everywhere.

**Distinctive physical characteristics.**   Geese and ducks both have webbed feet. Chickens are the smallest domesticated fowl. Turkeys have broad, fanlike tails.

**Habits.**   Chickens and turkeys adapt well to the tight living conditions in modern factory farms; ducks and geese need more space.

**Diet.**   Prepared poultry foods that supply needed nutrients.

Library of Congress Cataloging-in-Publication Data

Haggerty, Edward C., 1946-
    Farm Birds / Edward C. Haggerty.
        p.    cm. — (Nature's children)
    Includes index.
    Summary: Describes the physical characteristics, behavior, and
habitat of such birds as chickens and turkeys, focusing on those
found on farms.
    ISBN 0-7172-9079-4 (hardbound)
    1. Poultry-Juvenile literature.    [1. Poultry.]    I. Title
II. Series.
SF487.5.H34 1997
636.5—dc21

97-5947
CIP
AC

This library reinforced edition was published in 1997 exclusively by:

 **Grolier  Educational**

Sherman Turnpike, Danbury, Connecticut 06816

Set ISBN 0-7172-7661-9
Farm Birds ISBN 0-7172-9079-4

# Contents

Not very long ago at certain times of the year the skies of North America were crowded with wild ducks and geese. Millions of these birds filled the air as they migrated, or journeyed, from one part of the continent to another.

Among the wild ducks were mallards, pintails, and canvasbacks. There also were shovelers and wood ducks. And many kinds of geese, from the largest Canada goose to the smallest black brant, honked in V-formation across the skies.

Today, like chickens, most ducks and geese are farm birds. A few breeds are raised for show, but most are raised for their meat and eggs. Even the wily, wild turkey has, through careful breeding, been turned into a family-sized dinner bird.

Chickens, along with the domesticated breeds of ducks, geese, and turkeys, are called poultry. Different poultry farms tend to specialize in raising a particular kind of these birds. And they are raised not as pets but as food products.

*Along with chickens, geese, and turkeys, ducks, like this white muscovy, are valuable farm birds.*

# Down on the Farm

Years ago almost every family farm kept a flock of poultry. Some of these birds were for the family's own needs. But others were kept so that the meat and eggs could be sold for extra money.

Today, however, poultry farming—especially chicken farming—is big business. A single chicken house on a large, modern poultry farm can hold 40,000 chicks. These farms combine to sell more than 6 billion chickens each year.

Many of these large farms raise chickens for meat. Others raise them solely for their eggs. More than 68 billion eggs roll out of these egg farms during the year. Most eggs are sold for food, but some are kept for breeding more chickens.

On these huge farms everything happens fast. There isn't even time for hens to sit on their nests and hatch their chicks. Instead, farmers buy live chicks from suppliers. The chicks are then taken to the farm, where they are raised before being sent on to market. From hatchery to market takes no more than seven or eight weeks.

*Today a big poultry farm can raise up to 40,000 chickens at a time.*

# Who's a Chicken?

Among chickens names mean a lot. All very young chickens, for example, are called chicks. But young females also have a special name, pullets. Once they reach one year of age, females are called hens. Males are called roosters when they reach that age too.

Chickens have been domesticated—tamed and raised by people—for at least 4,000 years. Most modern chickens are descended from the red jungle fowl of southeast Asia.

Today chickens are bred even more carefully than ever, with breeders trying to create either heavy, fast-growing meat birds or good egg layers like the famous White Leghorn (farmers say "leggern").

There are even a few dual purpose birds, good for both meat and eggs. Among the best of these are the white Plymouth Rock and Wyandotte, the Rhode Island Red, and the New Hampshire. They all lay brown-shelled eggs.

*After they are a year old, male chickens—like this one—are called roosters.*

# Factory Fresh Eggs

On today's egg farms everything is organized and controlled. Egg-laying hens, for example, live indoors in wire-floored cages that are stacked up, four birds per cage. Artificial light and all-day access to feed and water encourage the chickens to lay eggs. These methods do such a good job that egg-farm hens lay as many as 250 eggs each year. (Wild birds usually produce just a single group of eggs each year.)

As the eggs are laid, they roll out of the cages and onto moving belts that take them to work areas. There the eggs are washed, graded, and packaged for market.

In today's chicken business special breeding farms (called hatcheries)—not individual hens —supply young chicks to the chicken farms. The eggs are hatched in incubators that keep them perfectly warm and moist. Machines even turn the eggs every few hours, just as a setting hen would— but more carefully!

When the chicks hatch, they are carefully cared for—and quickly shipped out to the chicken farms.

*Egg-laying is big business on some farms!*

# Caring for the Chicks

Baby chicks are delicate and need special care. In the wild it is the hens that take care of them. On a chicken farm the job is done by modern equipment.

As soon as the chicks arrive from the hatchery, the farmer puts them into a brooder, which is an enclosure used for raising young birds. A light bulb or heating element inside the brooder keeps the birds warm.

Feed and water for the chicks usually come from a hanging feeder. Flock owners generally buy their feed from local stores. The feed is rich in nutrients, and it is treated with medicines that can prevent the many diseases young chicks can catch.

Chicks leave the brooder when they are six weeks old. At that point farmers start letting them roost at night. When they roost, they sleep on a perch up off the ground. Birds are more comfortable on a perch. Roosting also keeps the birds from fouling their nest boxes, which are supposed to be used only for egg laying.

*Baby chicks often need special care.*

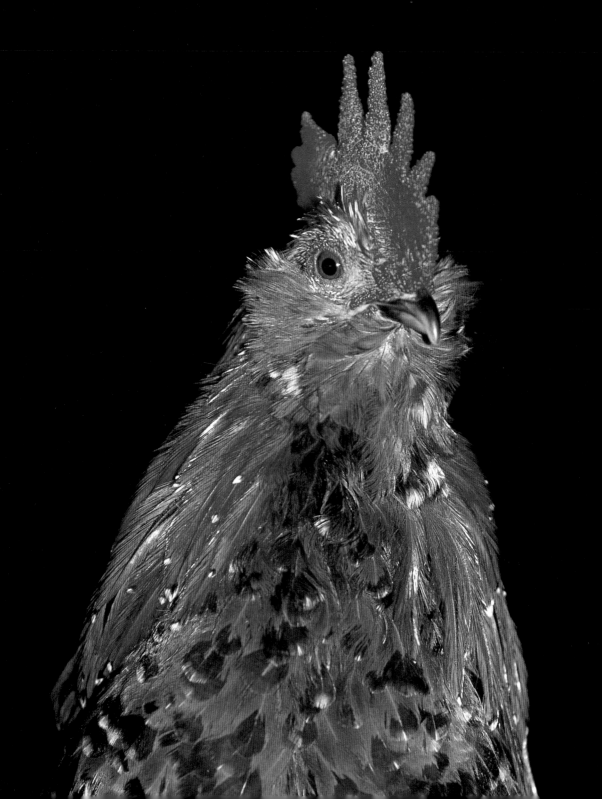

# Show Offs

Today the chicken industry is dominated by large farms. But young people in many parts of North America still raise poultry to show at county and state fairs.

At these poultry shows chickens are judged on their appearance according to standards set by the American Poultry Association (the APA). There are different standards for each recognized breed, and they include color, markings, plumage (feathers), and even shape of the comb on top of a chicken's head.

Bantam breeds, which are miniature versions of regular breeds, are popular show birds. Brahmins and Cochins—both miniature and full-sized—are also popular, mainly because of their thick, fluffy plumage and feathered shanks, or legs.

There also are fancy breeds with long necks and shanks and fewer feathers than most chickens. Among the most popular of these ornamental birds are the Polish fowl (which has a stunning crest of feathers), the downy-feathered Silky, and the ragged-looking Frizzle.

*Fancy breeds attract attention at poultry shows.*

# Wild Geese

Geese are web-footed water birds, members of the same family as swans and ducks. There are more than 35 different species of geese in the world, and 15 of them can be found in North America. The most common are the snow goose, the white-fronted goose, the brant, and the well-known Canada goose.

In the wild males and females often mate for life, with the males (called ganders) guarding the nest while the females sit on the eggs until they hatch. Parents fiercely defend their nests. Hissing and honking, they use their strong bills and wings to protect their eggs and babies, which are called goslings.

These birds find much of their food on land, and they enjoy eating grasses and grain. Their bills have toothlike grooves inside, which work like a strainer to let a bird push water from its mouth without pushing out food.

*Canada geese are among the most beautiful
and best known of all wild geese.*

# The Canada Goose

The sight of migrating Canada geese is thrilling. Honking loudly, they fly in a long, irregular V-formation. Their flapping wings create uplift for the geese behind them, making it easier for the geese to fly long distances. And fly long distances they do! Migrating Canada geese fly as far south as Mexico and as far north as the Arctic tundra.

A Canada goose is easy to recognize. There are several varieties, but all of them have brown bodies, black tails, heads, and necks, and large white patches running under the chin and up both cheeks. Fully grown, Canada geese weigh up to 17 pounds (8 kilograms) and have a wingspan of 6 feet (2 meters).

As a species, the Canada goose is thriving. In fact there are so many of them that some communities consider them pests. These large, aggressive birds take over lawns, parks, golf courses, or any other places that are safe from hunters. They scatter their droppings in the grass and boldly attack humans who try to shoo them away.

# Domestic Geese

In the old story "The Goose that Laid the Golden Egg" a farmer has a wonderful goose that can make people rich with eggs of solid gold. In truth, domestic geese are valuable not for gold but for their meat and feathers.

Goose meat is most popular in Europe, but even in North America it is a traditional holiday meal. In fact, farm geese are actually fed a special diet to fatten them up in the weeks just before holidays like Thanksgiving and Christmas. The geese usually are raised as free-range birds—not on factory farms— and are marketed when they are 10 to 13 weeks old and 10 to 12 pounds (4.5 to 5.4 kilograms).

The soft, fluffy underfeathers of some species of geese are particularly valuable. Light but amazingly warm, they make excellent insulation. So, several times each year farmers harvest the goose's underfeathers, which are called down. The down is carefully plucked from the live birds and then used to line clothing, sleeping bags, quilts, and pillows.

## Popular Breeds

There are several varieties of domestic geese, all of which are quite large. Among the best known is the Embden, which is an all-white breed that originally came from Germany. Another familiar breed is the African goose, a tall, gray bird that fattens very rapidly.

The common gray farm goose—found throughout North America—is actually the Toulouse breed. Named for a city in France, the Toulouse is popular because it is so hardy. It can withstand even the subzero winters of the Upper Midwest, where it is usually bred.

The usual farmyard variety of the Toulouse has a gray back, a light gray breast, and a white stomach. Show versions of the Toulouse, though, are fancier. They also are heavier. Carrying an extra five pounds (2.25 kilograms) or more, a show Toulouse is so heavy that its body actually drags on the ground.

*The common farm goose is hardy enough to withstand subzero winters.*

# Caring for Geese

Unlike chickens, most domestic geese are still raised on small farms just as they were long ago. In part this is because people simply do not eat as much goose meat as chicken. But it is also due to the nature of geese themselves.

Geese actually like to look for food. Indeed, they are happiest when they are allowed to wander around an area feeding all on their own.

To raise geese, farmers simply need an acre of pasture for every 20 to 40 geese. This pasture usually is enclosed with a wire fence. A simple shelter also is provided in case of bad weather. Some farmers clip the wings of their geese to keep them from flying away.

Geese are especially hardy animals. They are so healthy, in fact, that, unlike chickens, they don't need medicines added to their feed in order to stay healthy. They do, however, need a supply of grit, or gravel, nearby. Geese, like other birds, do not have teeth for chewing their feed, and this grit helps them digest their food.

*The African and the Tolouse are*
*popular breeds of geese.*

# Raising Goslings

Farmers usually buy their goslings from a hatchery that specializes in breeding geese. This saves the farmer the trouble of mating the birds and caring for the eggs.

After the goslings arrive at the farm, they move to a special brooding area. A separate building is not needed to brood, or raise, small numbers of geese. But the area does need to be warm, dry, and well lighted. Usually a 250-watt lamp provides enough heat to keep 25 goslings warm and comfortable.

The brooding area also needs to be well ventilated and free of drafts. The floor should be covered with wood shavings, chopped straw, or peat moss. This soaks up water and moisture. The floor must be kept clean and free of wet spots.

A pan or trough with a wire guard around it is used to hold water. The trough should be wide and deep enough for a gosling to dip in its bill and head, but it should be shallow enough to keep the gosling's whole body from falling inside. A gosling that gets wet and catches a chill can die.

*Goslings can be especially easy to raise.*

*Ducklings often get attention for their cute appearance.*

# Ducks

Like geese, ducks are web-footed water birds. About 40 different species of wild ducks live in North America.

In the air ducks are graceful and swift. In fact, they have been clocked at speeds of more than 70 miles (112 kilometers) an hour. They are equally graceful in the water, swimming and diving easily. On land, however, their awkward waddle can be quite amusing.

Ducks, like geese, are well suited to both water and cold weather. Their outer feathers are kept waterproof by an oil that comes from a gland near their tails. The birds spread this oil over their feathers as they primp and preen each day. Beneath these outerfeathers is an undercoat of soft, fluffy down that keeps the birds warm in just about any kind of weather.

After the breeding season ducks, like many birds, molt, losing all their flight feathers. Unlike most other birds, however, ducks actually are unable to fly for the three to four weeks it takes for their feathers to grow back.

# Dabblers

Have you ever seen a duck tip its head into the water and go bottom up? Its feet and tail jut into the air as it searches for food at the bottom of a shallow pond. Ducks that do this are dabblers, or pond ducks.

Dabblers live in marshes and shallow, fresh waters. Although dabblers mostly eat shellfish and insect larvae, some also eat water plants and insects.

The most common dabbler is the mallard. The male has a glossy green head, a white neckband, and a grayish-brown back. The female is a plainish spotty brown.

Two other dabblers are teals and northern shovelers. In North America you can find blue-winged, green-winged, and even cinnamon-colored teals. Northern shovelers can be identified by their flat, spoon-shaped bills.

*Green-headed mallards are the most*
*common of all North American dabblers.*

# Divers

Diving ducks (sometimes called divers, bay ducks, or sea ducks) make up another grouping of ducks. Ducks in this group live near large inland lakes and along the seacoast, where they find food by diving beneath the water. They eat water plants, snails, fish, shellfish, and insects.

Diving ducks are able to spend night after night far from shore on the open water. This helps them to migrate huge distances. Some species regularly fly from the northeastern United States as far south as Central and South America during the winter months.

One way to recognize diving ducks is the way they take flight. Dabblers take off with a quick upward leap. Diving ducks patter along the surface of the water for some distance until they take off.

*Ducks sometimes can be quite colorful.*

# Mergansers and Eiders

Mergansers (mer GAN serz) also belong to the group of diving ducks. They are fish-eating ducks that live in rivers, lakes, bays, and the sea. The common merganser (also called the goosander) and the hooded merganser are two fish-eating species common to North America.

A merganser's head has a small crest of feathers. Its large feet make it awkward on land but swift underwater. Its body is streamlined for faster swimming and diving.

Most ducks have broad, flat bills. Mergansers, however, have bills that are specially shaped for catching and holding live, slippery prey. Slender and narrow, the bill's tip is hooked, with saw-toothed ridges on the inside edges.

Eider ducks are another well-known kind of duck. They are especially prized for their down, which is collected from the nests and used in quilts and winter clothing.

*This muscovy drake (male) is quite a colorful character!*

# Farm-Raised Ducks

Most domestic ducks began, at some point in their history, as wild ducks. But years and years of careful breeding have transformed them into meaty food products. And, as duck meat has become more popular as a food, the duck industry in the United States has grown. Once located almost entirely on Long Island, in New York state, the industry has now spread to Wisconsin, Indiana, and Virginia.

The large, white-feathered Pekin is the most popular domestic breed because it reaches its market weight quickly. Like all domestic ducks except the muscovy, the Pekin originally was bred from the wild mallard. The voice of the female is a loud quack, while the male's voice is whispery.

The Rouen duck is popular for small farm flocks. It grows more slowly than the Pekin, so it costs more in feed to raise it. Rouens have the same color pattern as the wild mallard.

*Ducks have been a part of life on the farm for many, many years.*

*Sometimes, domestic ducks are raised in cages, the way chickens are.*

# Caring for Ducks

Like geese, ducks are raised on a smaller scale than chickens. In general, most come from fairly small farms.

Pekin ducks are ready for market when they are seven to nine weeks old. Rouens and other domestic ducks take a bit longer to mature—twenty weeks or so. These short growing times mean that farmers who raise ducks during the late spring can let the flocks find their own food outdoors.

Ducks are not as good as geese at finding their own food. But still, farmers rarely have to provide spring-raised birds with more than a lush green field. The birds' wings are usually clipped to keep them from flying away. Beyond this, there is little to do to have the ducks ready for market by late summer or early fall.

Not all ducks are raised in the spring, however. Since ducks raised in other seasons will not necessarily have enough natural food available, farmers generally need to give them additional things to eat. Some farmers buy special duck feed, while others simply add extra cracked corn to chicken feed.

# Raising Ducklings

Pekin ducks are what is known as poor setters. This means that they often neglect their eggs. As a result, farmers sometimes put duck eggs under chicken hens to hatch. The hens, which have an instinct to set on eggs, usually will accept the eggs and handle them as if they were their own.

Ducks are often brooded in special, warm areas, just as baby chicks are. A 250-watt light bulb will supply enough heat for 30 ducklings. Ducklings grow faster than chicks, though, and will soon outgrow a small space.

Like all waterfowl, ducks like to dip their heads under water to wash their faces and bills. Water troughs usually are set up—with wire guards in place—to keep the ducklings from falling in.

Ducks, like geese, do not catch many of the common diseases that can harm chickens and turkeys. So, farmers do not have to give ducklings medicated feed, which could, in fact, be harmful to them.

*Ducks can even make good playmates!*

# Turkeys

One of the most unusual looking of all birds, turkeys have long been a part of North American feasts and festivals. In years gone by, wild birds were hunted and brought to the table as a sign of the hunter's skill. Today, birds generally come from large turkey farms. But the steaming roast turkey is no less prized today than it was three hundred years ago.

Wild turkeys usually live near swamps or deep in woods and brush lands. During the day they search about for nuts, seeds, plants, berries, and insects. At night they roost in trees.

The male, or tom, turkey has greenish-bronze feathers with golden highlights. From its chin hang folds of skin called wattles. A tuft of hairlike feathers hangs beardlike from its chest. The female (the hen) has dull-colored feathers. Both male and female have a reddish head and neck, which are bare and wrinkled.

Turkeys are surprisingly good fliers, given their size and weight. But when threatened they usually prefer to escape by running.

*Wild turkeys usually live near swamps or deep in woods or brush lands.*

# How the Turkey Got Its Name

Turkey is an odd name for a bird that is native to North and Central America. Some people think it got its name from the sound of one of its calls, a soft "turk, turk, turk."

Another likely idea is that, in the past, people confused it with another bird—the guinea fowl. Hundreds of years ago African birds called guinea fowl were imported into Europe through Turkey. These large, plump birds were sometimes called Turkey hens. Along the way, people may have picked up the name and used it for the native American bird.

Today, all domestic turkeys come from a Mexican ancestor. When Spanish soldiers conquered Mexico in 1519, they found that the Aztec people were raising domesticated turkeys. The Spanish took some of these birds back to Europe with them. Later, English colonists brought some of these same domestic turkeys to North America, bringing the turkey back to its place of beginning!

# Domestic Turkeys

Like geese and ducks, domestic turkeys are raised almost exclusively for their meat. Once served mainly on holidays, turkey has gotten much more popular in recent years. Meaty, low in fat, and fairly economical to buy, it is a popular food source on North American tables.

In many areas farmers still keep a few turkeys in farmyard flocks. Most of these birds get their wings clipped to keep them from flying away. Still, they sometimes manage to wander from home and breed freely with wild turkeys.

Mass-production farms raise, house, and process turkeys in much the same way as chickens. As with chickens, speed is the main goal. In one of these factory farms turkeys are ready for market at 16 to 22 weeks of age.

Selective breeding has produced domestic turkeys that are quite large. A fully grown Beltsville small white can weigh up to 22 pounds (10 kg). The broad-breasted Bronze can weigh up to 36 pounds (16.2 kg).

## Raising Turkeys

Given their size and wild origin, you might expect turkeys to be hardy, easy-to-raise birds. But that is not the case. Poults, or baby turkeys, are delicate and require special care. They need to be kept warm and dry for several weeks after hatching. If they are rained on or walk in wet grass, they can become seriously ill.

Farmers usually buy live poults from a hatchery. Because poults younger than five days old sometimes neglect to eat and drink, farmers usually have to set up brooding areas. Here the newborn poults are forced to stay near heat, water, and feed.

Poults also tend to eat the litter used for covering the floor of the cages. This can plug up a bird's gizzard, or lower stomach, and can cause the bird to lose weight or even die. So poults need to be fed grit to help them break down the litter into a digestible form.

Turkey droppings release ammonia, which can cause lung problems and harmful breast blisters. For this reason, turkey barns need good ventilation and frequent cleaning.

*Today turkeys are raised by the thousands
on large-scale farms.*

# Turkey: The Bird of Feasts

Did you know that Benjamin Franklin favored the turkey over the eagle as the national bird? Franklin thought this because wild turkeys had been given to the Pilgrims by Native Americans for the first Thanksgiving feast.

Tradition has it that the first Thanksgiving was held in 1621, given by the Pilgrims at Plymouth to celebrate their harvest. Governor Bradford invited Chief Massasoit, who brought 90 people and stayed three days! The banquet menu included turkey, venison (deer meat), oysters, clams, corn cakes, and boiled pumpkin.

In truth, the "first" Thanksgiving actually took place in the late fall of 1619 at the Berkeley Plantation in Virginia! There the colonists held a prayer service to honor their arrival in the New World. Based on the foods available at that time and place, the menu for the feast may well have included Chesapeake oysters, roasted quail, and bacon . . . but no turkey!

Today, however, turkey is pretty much the bird of choice for Thanksgiving. In fact, in the United States people eat 45 million turkeys on Thanksgiving Day!

# Words to Know

**Bantam**   A physically small breed of fowl or often a miniature version of a standard breed.

**Broiler**   A chicken sold as meat.

**Brooder**   A special room or area in a barn used to raise newly hatched birds. The brooder provides water, feed, and warmth.

**Chick**   A baby chicken, either male or female.

**Down**   An underlayer of soft, fluffy feathers.

**Drake**   A male duck.

**Gander**   A male goose.

**Gosling**   A baby goose.

**Hen**   A year-old female chicken or turkey.

**Migration**   Seasonal travel to and from the breeding area.

**Molt**   To shed feathers.

**Plumage**   The feathers of birds.

**Poult**   A young turkey.

**Poultry**   The domesticated breeds of chickens, ducks, turkeys, and geese.

**Pullet**   A female chicken less than a year old.

**Rooster**   A year-old male chicken.

**Tom**   A male turkey.

# INDEX

**Cover Photo:** Lynn M. Stone
**Photo Credits:** Norvia Behling (Behling & Johnson Photography), pages 8, 13, 26, 35, 41;
D. DeMello (Wildlife Conservation Society), page 38; Lynn M. Stone, pages 4, 14, 20, 23, 33, 45;
SuperStock, Inc., pages 7, 11, 17, 29, 31, 36; Wildlife Conservation Society, page 25.